The
Little
Brown Girl

A Collection of
Affirmations from A to Z

WRITTEN BY
AMIRA-JAY FARRAR

ILLUSTRATED BY
SONIA SEKELOVA

Amira-Jay Farrar

Copyright©2020 The Little Brown Girl (I Am The Little Brown Girl)
Amira-Jay Farrar

All rights reserved.

ISBN 10: 8576488490
ISBN 13: 9798576488490

No part of this book may be reproduced or transmitted in any form or by any means, electronic or mechanical, including photocopying, recording, or by any information storage and retrieval system, without permission in writing from the copyright owner. Any people or images provided by the illustrators are models and clipart and such images are being used for illustrative purposes only. Certain imagery print information available in the back of this book.

Amira-Jay Farrar

THE LITTLE BROWN GIRL

I Am The Little Brown Girl

DEDICATED

To Amira-Jay & All The Little Brown Girls

Little Brown Girl beautiful as ever, who shows no fear.
You are favored, you are divine, always remember God is near.

Little Brown Girl so strong, so confident and oh so wise,
Sweet Princess it is okay to be who you are no need to apologize.

Little Brown Girl you are smart, you are cute, and your smile can light up a room. Your skin color, clothes, dreads, and natural hair styles are not a threat or a costume. Truth be told, that is what those that are intimidated by your Melanin are likely to Assume.

Little Brown Girl always remember that you are fearfully and wonderfully made carefully created in the image of God, God is Love so there is no room for others to throw shade.

Take a look around and by all means please do not whisper and frown. It's Her, **The Little Brown Girl** who refuse to accept or be called an offensive noun.

The Little Brown Girl growing up in every community, city, state, yes, even in your town

©2020 By Corliss Meredith

With Love Always & Forever
Author, Corliss Meredith

THE LITTLE BROWN GIRL

Amira-Jay Farrar

Victorious
Successful
Ambitious
Incredible
Fearless
Gifted
Terrific
Loving
Joyful
Beautiful
Kind
Worthy
Necessary
Determined
X-Factor
Qualified
Zealous
Hard Working
Unique
Phenomenal
Courageous
Magnificent
Eloquent
Remarkable
Outstanding
Yes, I Can

I Am The Little Brown Girl

INTRODUCTION

The I AM affirmations were inspired by Amira-Jay feeling left out when she was not chosen to attend a private school in Los Angeles, California; leading her to say they probably did not pick me because I was the only brown girl. That then inspired her mom to let her know that she is brown, beautiful, smart, and strong.
So, every morning she wakes up and looks in the mirror saying,

"I am beautiful, I am smart, I am strong".

Amira-Jay wants to also empower other little brown girls by letting them know that the I AM affirmations was created to let them know that they can be all the things they ever imagine to be because they have all things within. Amira-Jay also wants YOU to know that YOU are everything that you can ever imagine. Dream Big Princess and leave a little glitter, sparkle, and SHINE Bright. Know that your *Melanin* is what sets you apart and makes you stand out beautifully. As you look in the mirror each day, know that you are

"beautiful, smart, and strong".

THE LITTLE BROWN GIRL

I Am The Little Brown Girl

I Am An Ambitious
Little Brown Girl

Ambitious
Having or showing a strong desire to succeed.

I Am A Beautiful
Little Brown Girl

Beautiful
Delightful to see, hear, or experience; lovely to the senses; having beauty.

I Am The Little Brown Girl

I Am A Courageous
Little Brown Girl

Courageous
Brave; bold; Fearless.

I Am The Little Brown Girl

I Am A Determined
Little Brown Girl

Determined
To Decide. Strong-minded; to bring about; produce.

I Am The Little Brown Girl

I Am An Eloquent
Little Brown Girl

Eloquent
Graceful. Using words well, in a way that others enjoy hearing or reading.

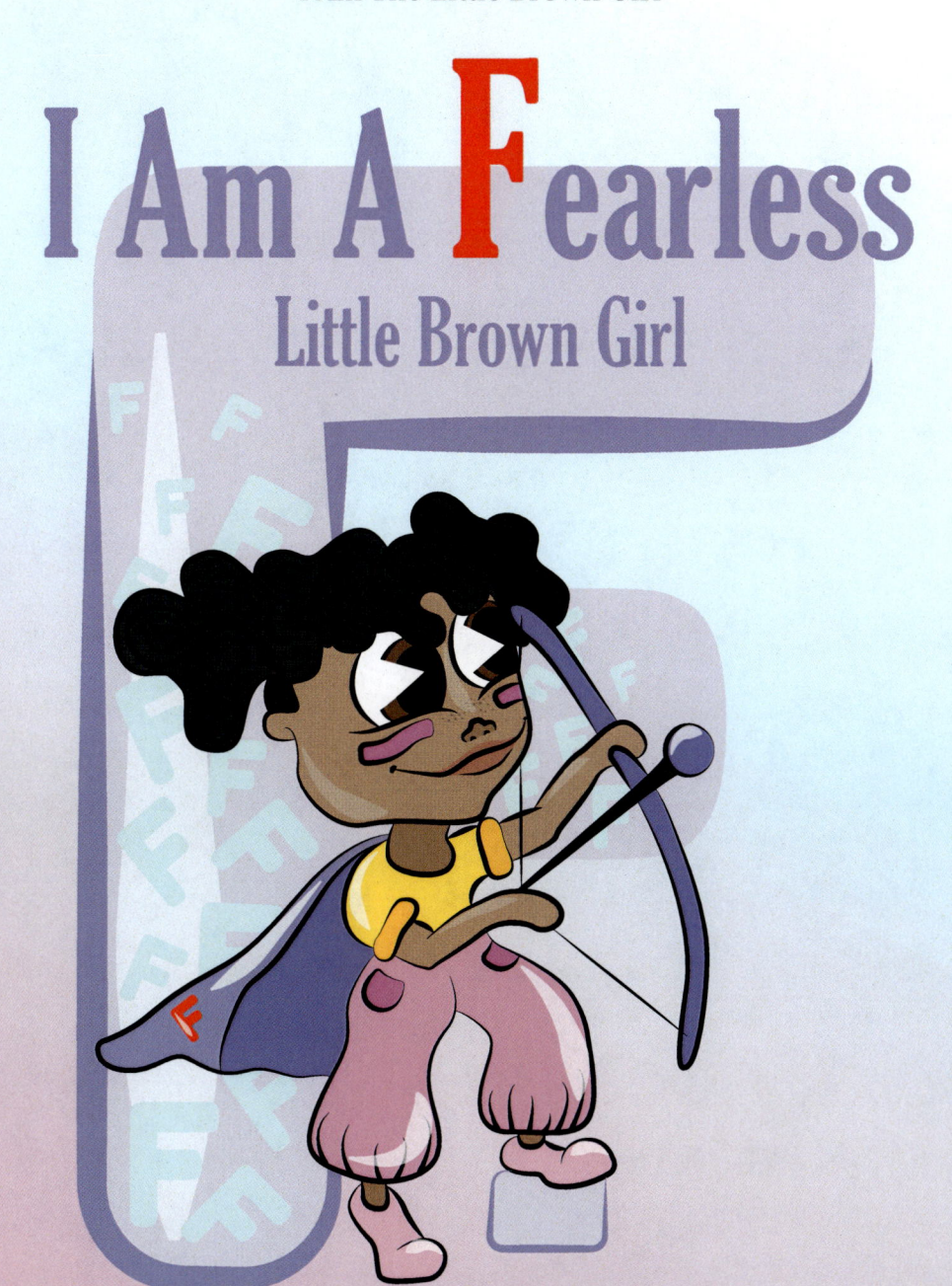

I Am A Fearless
Little Brown Girl

Fearless
Courageous. Without fear; brave.

I Am The Little Brown Girl

I Am A Gifted
Little Brown Girl

Gifted
Having a special talent or ability.

I Am The Little Brown Girl

I Am A Hard Working
Little Brown Girl

Hard Working
Diligent. Thorough. To work very hard.

I Am The Little Brown Girl

I Am An Incredible
Little Brown Girl

Incredible
Amazing. Astonishing. Wonderful.

I Am The Little Brown Girl

I Am A Joyful
Little Brown Girl

Joyful
Feeling, showing, or causing great happiness; glad; happy.

I Am The Little Brown Girl

I Am A Kind
Little Brown Girl

Kind
Helpful; friendly; good.

I Am The Little Brown Girl

I Am A Loving
Little Brown Girl

Loving
Strong feelings of affection for another person.

I Am The Little Brown Girl

I Am A Magnificent
Little Brown Girl

Magnificent
The quality of being grand or splendid.

I Am The Little Brown Girl

I Am A Necessary
Little Brown Girl

Necessary
Needed; not able to be put aside.

I Am The Little Brown Girl

I Am An Outstanding
Little Brown Girl

Outstanding
Standing out from others because of high quality; excellent.

I Am The Little Brown Girl

I Am A Phenomenal
Little Brown Girl

Phenomenal
Amazing or Extraordinary.

I Am The Little Brown Girl

I Am A Qualified
Little Brown Girl

Qualified
Skilled. Having the qualities or skills that are needed.

I Am The Little Brown Girl

I Am A Remarkable
Little Brown Girl

Remarkable
Unusual or exceptional. Worthy of being noticed or mentioned.

I Am The Little Brown Girl

I Am A Successful
Little Brown Girl

Successful
Flourishing; thriving; triumphant. Accomplishing an aim or purpose. Ending or doing well.

I Am The Little Brown Girl

I Am A Terrific
Little Brown Girl

Terrific
Much greater than the ordinary or usual. Very good; fantastic.

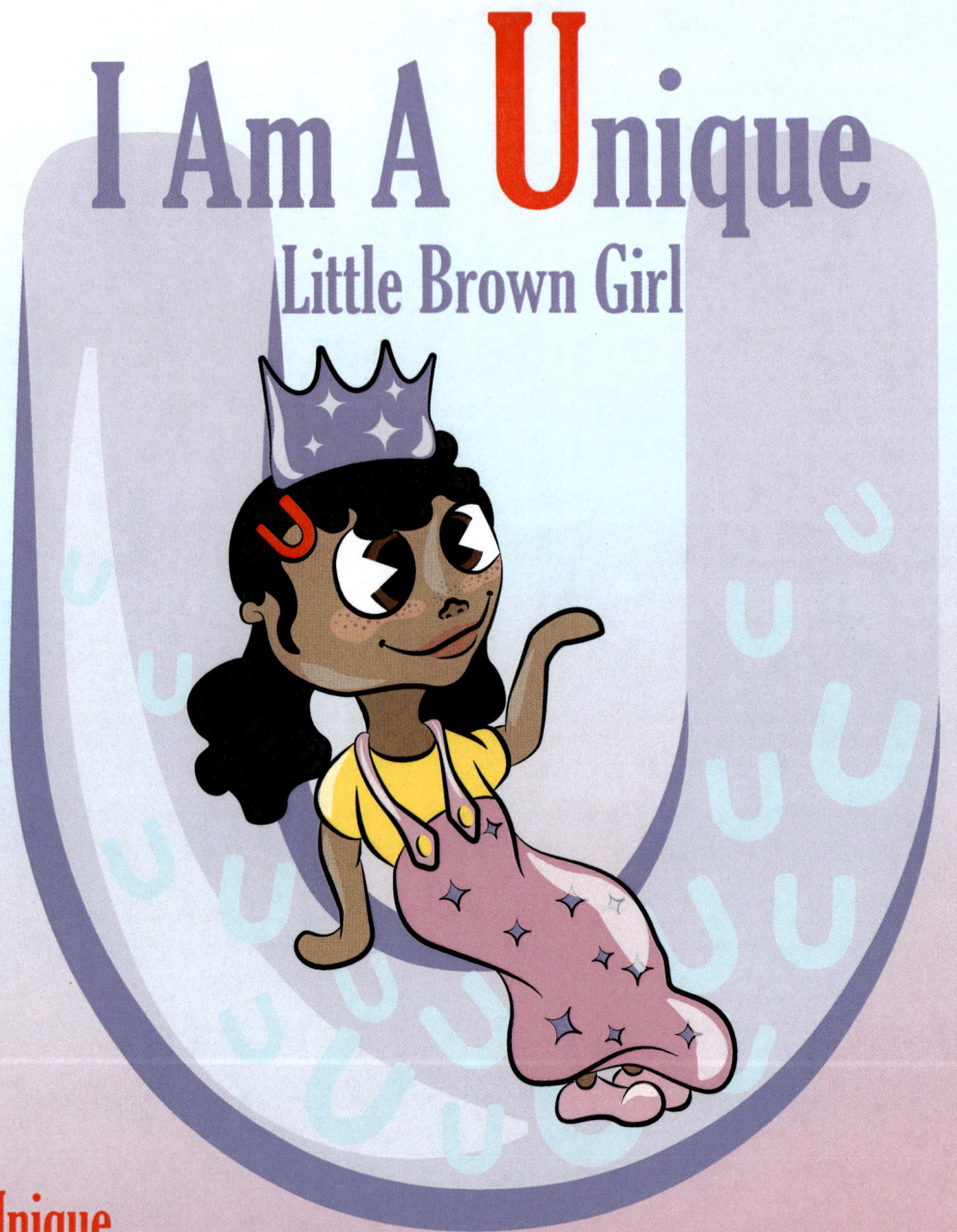

I Am The Little Brown Girl

I Am A Unique
Little Brown Girl

Unique
Exceptional. having no equal; different from everything else. being the only one of its type.

I Am The Little Brown Girl

I Am A Victorious
Little Brown Girl

Victorious
Winning. Having won a victory.

I Am The Little Brown Girl

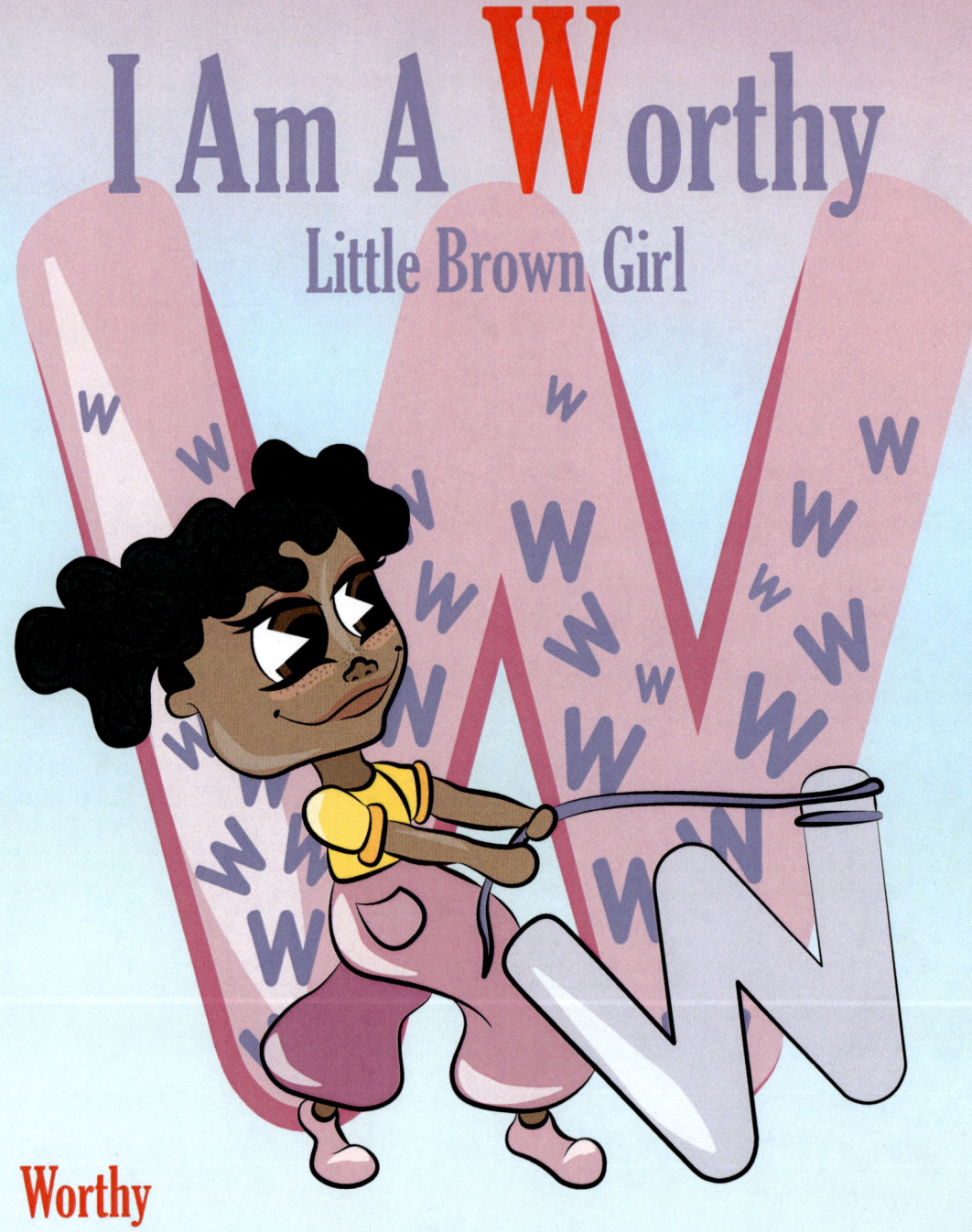

I Am A Worthy
Little Brown Girl

Worthy
Deserving. Having enough worth or value.

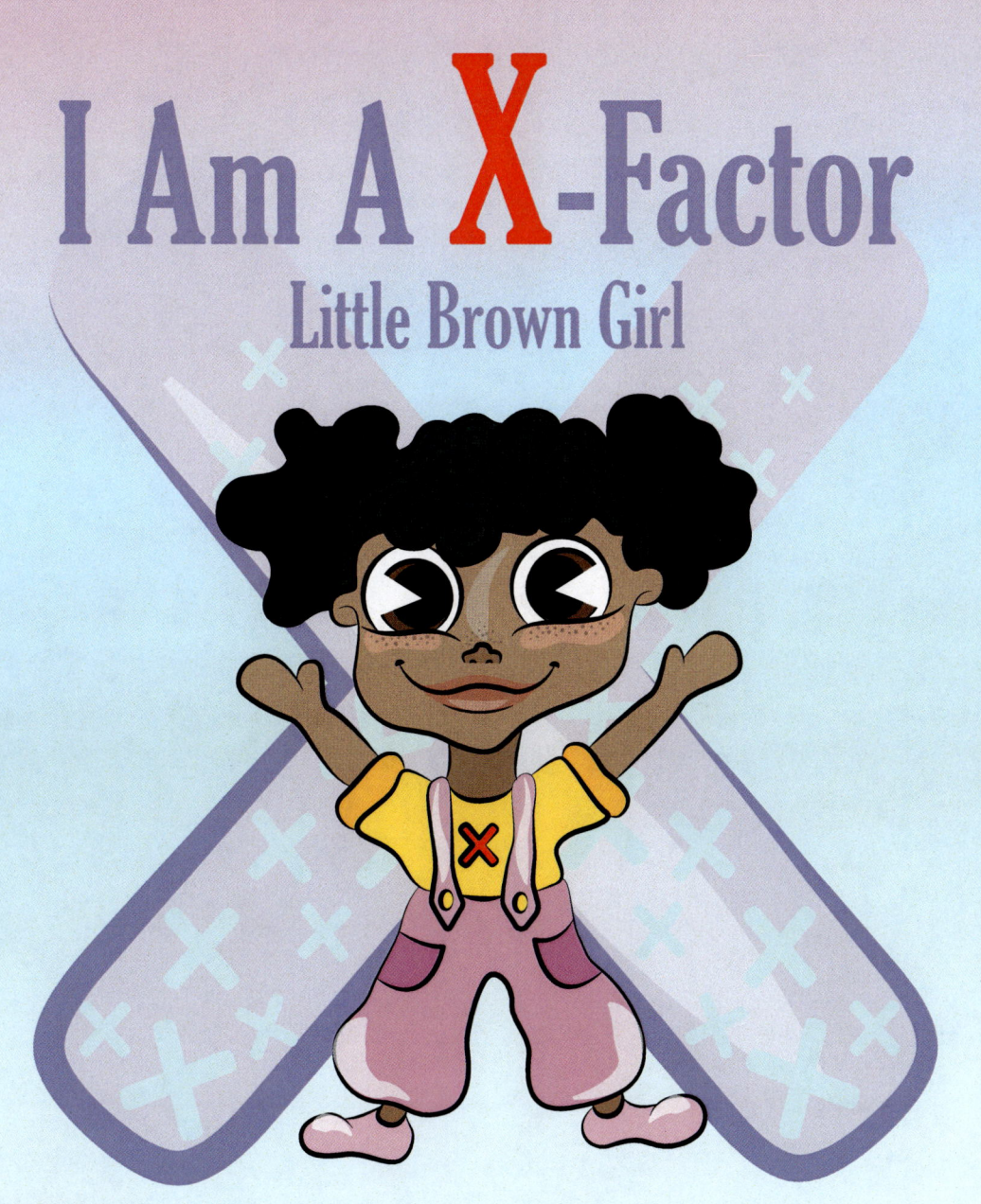

I Am The Little Brown Girl

I Am A X-Factor
Little Brown Girl

X-Factor
A remarkable special talent or quality. It is a set of unique qualities that differentiate a person from everyone else.

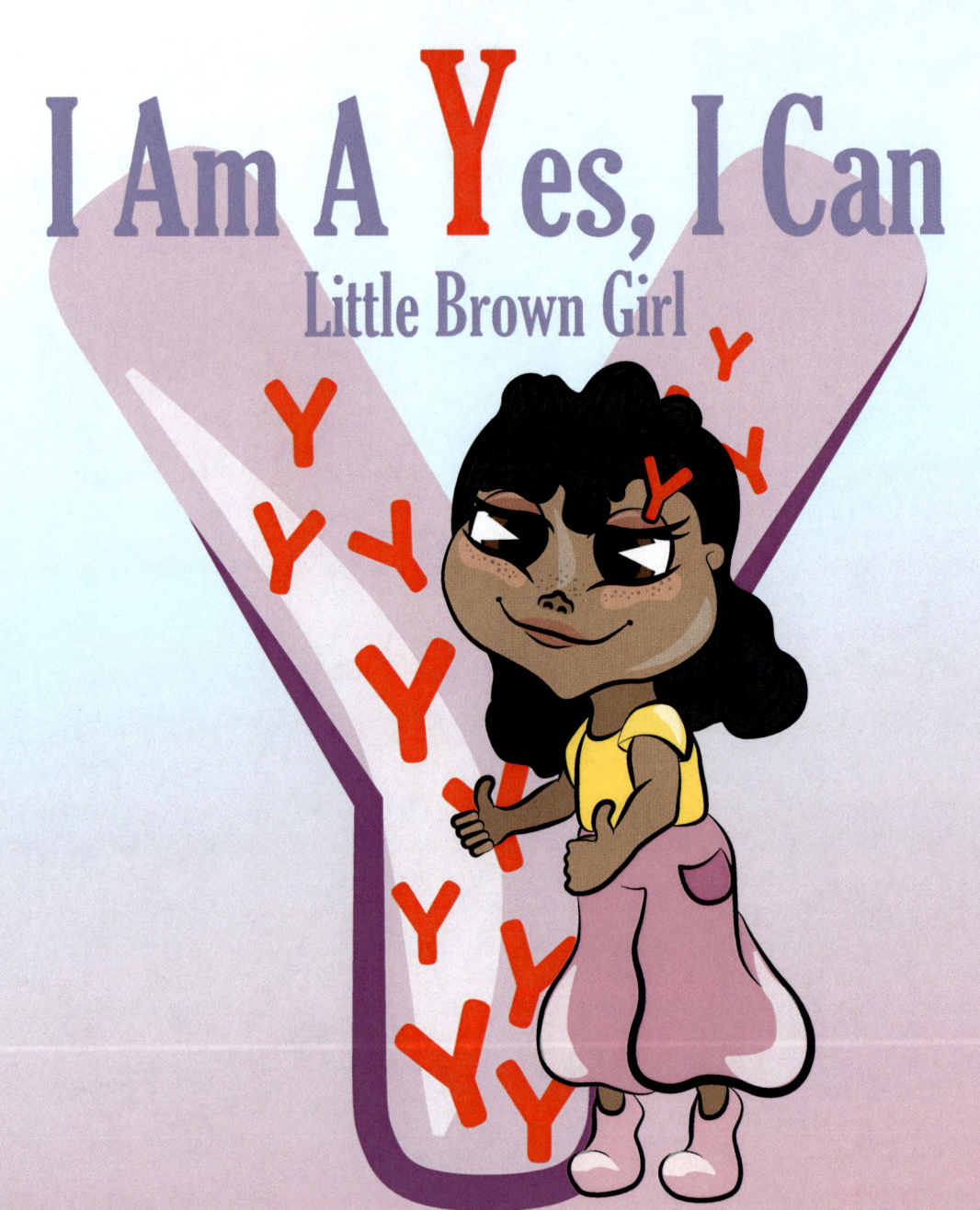

I Am The Little Brown Girl

I Am A Yes, I Can
Little Brown Girl

Yes, I Can
Determined. Sure thing. To be able to; have the ability to.

I Am The Little Brown Girl

I Am A Zealous
Little Brown Girl

Zealous
Eager. Showing, or filled with an intense enthusiasm, as toward a cause, purpose, or activity.

Amira-Jay Farrar

Repeat These Words I Invite You To Say,
Amira's Little Brown Girl A To Z Affirmations From Day To Day

I Am Ambitious
I Am Beautiful
I Am Courageous
I Am Determined
I Am Eloquent
I Am Fearless
I Am Gifted

I Am Hard Working
I Am Incredible
I Am Joyful
I Am Kind
I Am Loving
I Am Magnificent
I Am Necessary

I Am Outstanding
I Am Phenomenal
I Am Qualified
I Am Remarkable
I Am Successful
I Am Terrific

I Am Unique
I Am Victorious
I Am Worthy
I Am X-Factor
Yes, I Can
I Am Zealous

I Am The Little Brown Girl

THE LITTLE
BROWN GIRL

I Am The Little Brown Girl

I AM THE LITTLE BROWN GIRL

I Am The Little Brown Girl
Who Embraces Her Magnificent Melanin And Flawless Skin Tone
I Am Confident, Outspoken, And Not Afraid To Make It Known.

I Am The Little Brown Girl who Refuse To Accept Or Be Recognized As An offensive Noun
I am Black
I am Bold
I am confident
Why "Talking" I am Still A Child

Where Is The Love? You Know Name Calling Is Wrong
This Little Black Girl Will Soon Grow Up To Be Successful And Strong
And Not To Be Mistaken As Wild, Underrated, Or Just Another Sad Song.
Soon I Will Be An Adult A Daughter Of God The Almighty King. Who Loves Me And Recognizes Me As Princess Or Even As His Queen.

I Affirm, The Little Brown Girl Is The Name I Chose
However, In Order To Get To The Conclusion of the Matter, I Must Disclose
The Reason My Smile Lights Up A Room, Is Because I Am Fearless,
And I Am Becoming, So Please Step back And Allow Me To Bloom.
Go Ahead Say It My Friend It's Simply Okay. The Little Brown Girl Is A Name That I Am Proud To Be Called Each And Every Day.

©2020 By Corliss Meredith

THE LITTLE BROWN GIRL

Amira-Jay Farrar

ABOUT THE AUTHOR

Amira-Jay Farrar
Amira-Jay is a gifted and talented 6-year-old that considers herself to be brown. She is wise beyond her years. She is this little big person that is very passionate about people.

Amira-Jay loves to bake and watch Life Hacks. Her family and friends have discovered that she is the youngest seamstress that they know. Amira-Jay is always up for any challenge and very confident that she will succeed and try her best.

With a YES, I CAN Determination; This Little Brown Girl can even get a seat in the White House!

THE LITTLE BROWN GIRL

I Am The Little Brown Girl

STAY CONNECTED WITH AMIRA-JAY FARRAR

Face Book
Iamthelittlebrowngirl

Instagram
@iamthelittlebrowngirl
_amirajay

SUBSCRIBE TO AMIRA'S YOUTUBE CHANNEL

I Am The Little Brown Girl

STAY IN TOUCH WITH AMIRA

Email:
iamthelittlebrowngirl@gmail.com

Website:
www.iamthelittlebrowngirl.com

Ready Writers
Publishing Enterprise & Consulting

Amira-Jay Farrar

Illustration and Book Cover Creator
Sonia Sekelova
@haha_sklv

Definitions: https://kids.wordsmyth.net/we/

Collaboration & Self-publishing Manager
Mom, Ashley Polk

Publisher: Corliss Meredith

Publishing Information
Ready Writers Publishing Enterprise & Consulting

Published in the United States by
Ready Writers Publishing Enterprise & Consulting

Pflugerville, Texas

Poems: The Little Brown Girl ©2020 Written By: Corliss Meredith
©2020 The Little Brown Girl (I Am The Little Brown Girl)

A catalog record for this book is available from the Library of Congress
ISBN 9798576488490

Printed and bound by:
The book Patch & Print On Demand Services

Make It Your Goal To Leave A Lasting Legacy With Your Words Worldwide

Corliss Meredith

www.readywriterpublishingenterprise.com

Made in the USA
Monee, IL
18 December 2022